CONTENTS

TransFormers ARMADA

Pedigree®

Published by Pedigree Books Limited
Beech Hill House, Walnut Gardens, Exeter, Devon EX4 4DG.
E-mail books@pedigreegroup.co.uk
Published 2003

£6.99

...TAKING THEM APART AND PUTTING THEM BACK TOGETHER AGAIN... **REWIRED** TO **THEIR** LIKING.

WITH THIS NEW REWIRING THE DECEPTICONS FOUND THEY COULD FUSE OUR SMALLER BODIES TO THEIR OWN...

RRROOOAARRRGH!!

...AND THAT BY DOING SO THEIR OWN POWERS GREATLY **INCREASED.**

SO NOW THEY'RE ON A RAMPAGE. A RAMPAGE TO CAPTURE AS MANY MINI-CONS AS THEY CAN. WHO KNOWS WHAT THEY PLAN TO DO WITH ALL THAT NEW POWER?

YOU THINK WE'LL END UP GETTING... **REWIRED?**

ALL I **DO** KNOW IS THAT WE'RE NOT GOING DOWN WITHOUT A FIGHT.

WE'RE FINISHED!!

BUT IF YOUR FRIEND GOT CAUGHT THEN HOW--?

...SAY LONGARM?

->SIGH<- WHAT?

ARE YOU... ARE YOU SCA--?

WE **ALL** ARE JOLT.

FINISHED!!

LUCKILY HE ESCAPED. I HEARD HE'S ON THE RUN NOW... WITH A GANG OF OTHER MINI-CONS WHO ESCAPED

14

...UH OH.

I-I... I DON'T UNDERSTAND... IT *SHOULD'VE* WORKED...

BEEP

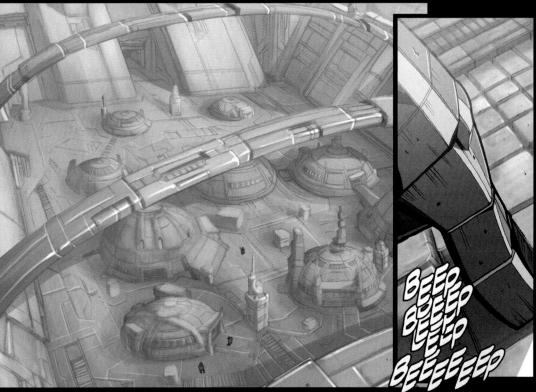

BEEP
BEEEP
EEP
BEEEEEEP

OUTTA THE WAY!

UNH!

TONK!

BZZMMMM

NOTHING.

YEAH... SURE.

...M-M-MAYBE THEY T-TURNED B-BACK...

DON'T LOOK BACK! JUST RUN!!

HEY!

...WHERE DO YOU THINK YOU'RE GOING?

VVIP

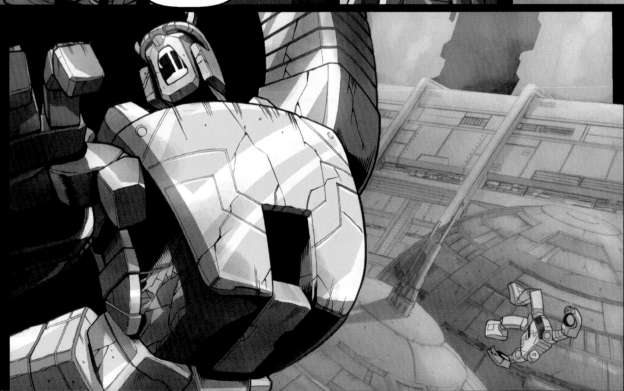

THUD!

NOT A BAD DAY FOR THE HUNT, EH *DEMOLISHOR?*

NOT BAD AT ALL.

RADIO *MEGATRON* AT HEADQUARTERS. LET HIM KNOW WE'RE DONE HERE.

DECEPTICON HEADQUARTERS.

ATTENTION MEGATRON. DO YOU READ?

SPEAK.

VILLAGE TAKEOVER IS COMPLETE. THIS WAS THE LAST OF THEM. WHAT DO WE DO NEXT?

NEXT?

HELLO? ANYBODY **HOME** IN THERE?...

RESTORING AUDIO PARAMETERS

...**WAIT**...HE'S MOVING. I THINK HE'S COMING TO...

YEP.

UH HUH.

...**GOOD**. FOR A WHILE THERE I THOUGHT WE WERE TOO LATE. LOOKS LIKE HE'S GOING TO MAKE IT AFTER ALL...

AGREED.

DEFINITELY.

RESTORING OPTICS

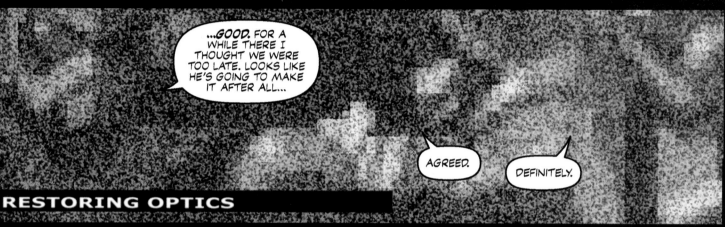

...SAY, WHAT **IS** YOUR NAME ANYWAY?

NEED A NAME.

GOTTA HAVE A NAME.

...WELCOME BACK TO REALITY, **UMMMM**...

...UHNN... S-SPARKPLUG... NAME'S **SPARKPLUG**.

...W-WHERE AM I? WHO ARE Y--?

ALL RIGHT **SPARKPLUG**, SORRY TO HAVE TO DO THIS BUT...

HEY! WHAT THE--?!

WHAT ARE YOU DOING?!

DON'T MOVE. THIS'LL ONLY TAKE A SECOND.

DECEPTICON HEADQUARTERS.

...Y-YOU THINK WE'RE GETTING IN TH-*THERE*?

DON'T WORRY, IT'S NOT AS TOUGH AS IT LOOKS...

"...THE HARDEST PART IS GETTING PAST THE MOTION BLASTERS. ALL WE HAVE TO DO IS CREATE A DISTRACTION SO WE CAN SNEAK PAST THEM."

AND HOW, MIGHT I ASK, DO YOU INTEND TO DO THAT?

OHHHH NO... YOU HAVE *GOT* TO BE KIDDING. UH UH. *NO WAY.* NO, NO, NO, NO--

33

ALRIGHT MINI-CONS...

...LET'S GET FREE.

CYBER CITY.

DOOOM!

HA! HA! HA! HA! HA!

TONK!

...PRIM...
UNNHH... WE...
WE'RE NO MATCH
FOR THEM... THE...
THE MINI-CONS
MAKE THEM TOO
STRONG

...WHAT
SHOULD WE
D-DO...

...IF...
IF WE STAY
HERE... W-WE
DIE...

...IF WE WANT
TO SAVE... SAVE
CYBERTRON WE HAVE
TO STAY ALIVE... I...
THINK THERE'S ONLY
ONE CHOICE...

...RETREAT
AND
REGROUP.

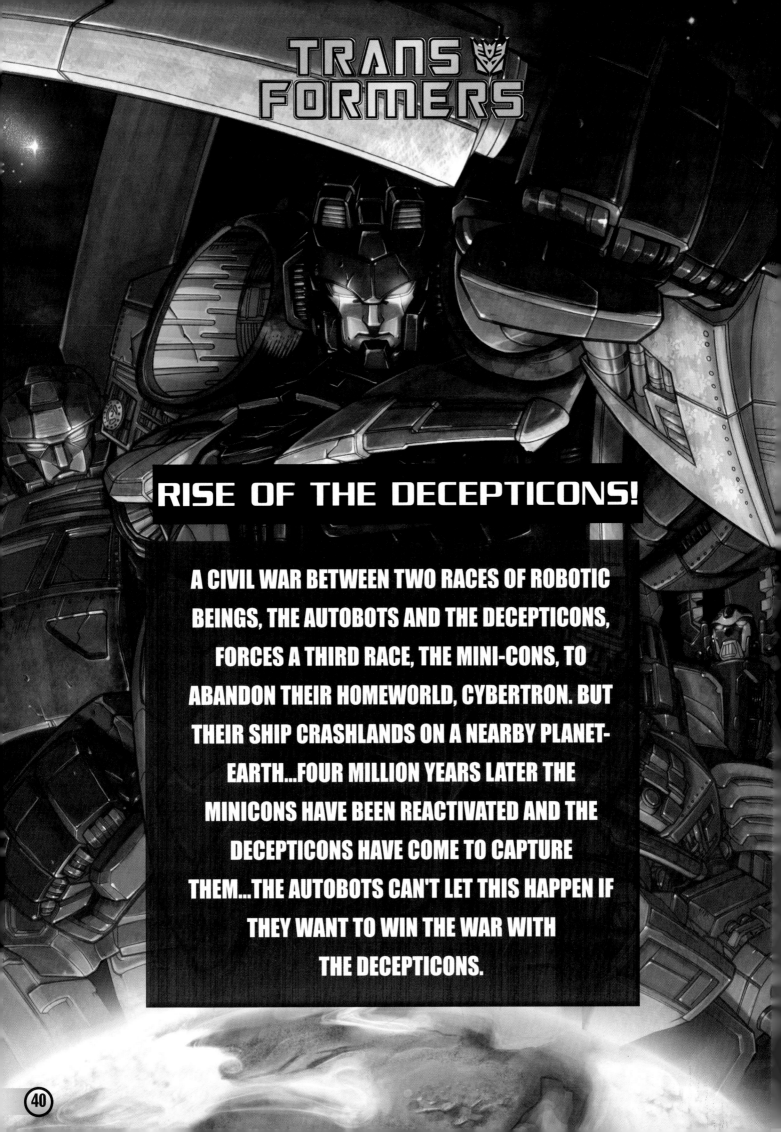

TRANSFORMERS

RISE OF THE DECEPTICONS!

A CIVIL WAR BETWEEN TWO RACES OF ROBOTIC BEINGS, THE AUTOBOTS AND THE DECEPTICONS, FORCES A THIRD RACE, THE MINI-CONS, TO ABANDON THEIR HOMEWORLD, CYBERTRON. BUT THEIR SHIP CRASHLANDS ON A NEARBY PLANET—EARTH...FOUR MILLION YEARS LATER THE MINICONS HAVE BEEN REACTIVATED AND THE DECEPTICONS HAVE COME TO CAPTURE THEM...THE AUTOBOTS CAN'T LET THIS HAPPEN IF THEY WANT TO WIN THE WAR WITH THE DECEPTICONS.

PEACHY.

YOU... *IDIOT!* YOU COULD'VE BEEN HURT.

WORSE, YOU COULD HAVE HURT *ME!* THAT STUNT WAS RECKLESS, BRAINDEAD, IRRESPONSIBLE.

YOUR POINT?

ER, GUYS...

WE'VE GOT COMPANY-- IT'S THE *AUTOBOTS.*

WHAT BRINGS YOU UP HERE, *OPTIMUS PRIME?* SOME WORLD-SHATTERING THREAT... I HOPE.

ACTUALLY, CARLOS...

...WE'VE COME TO SAY GOODBYE.

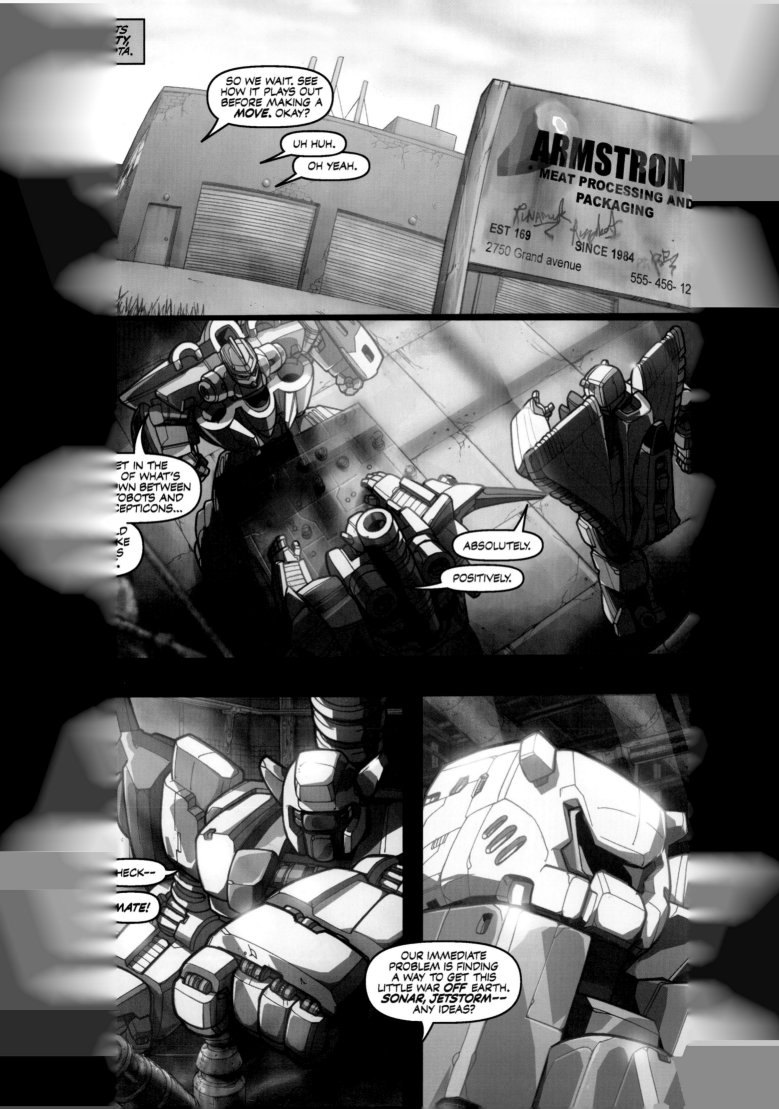

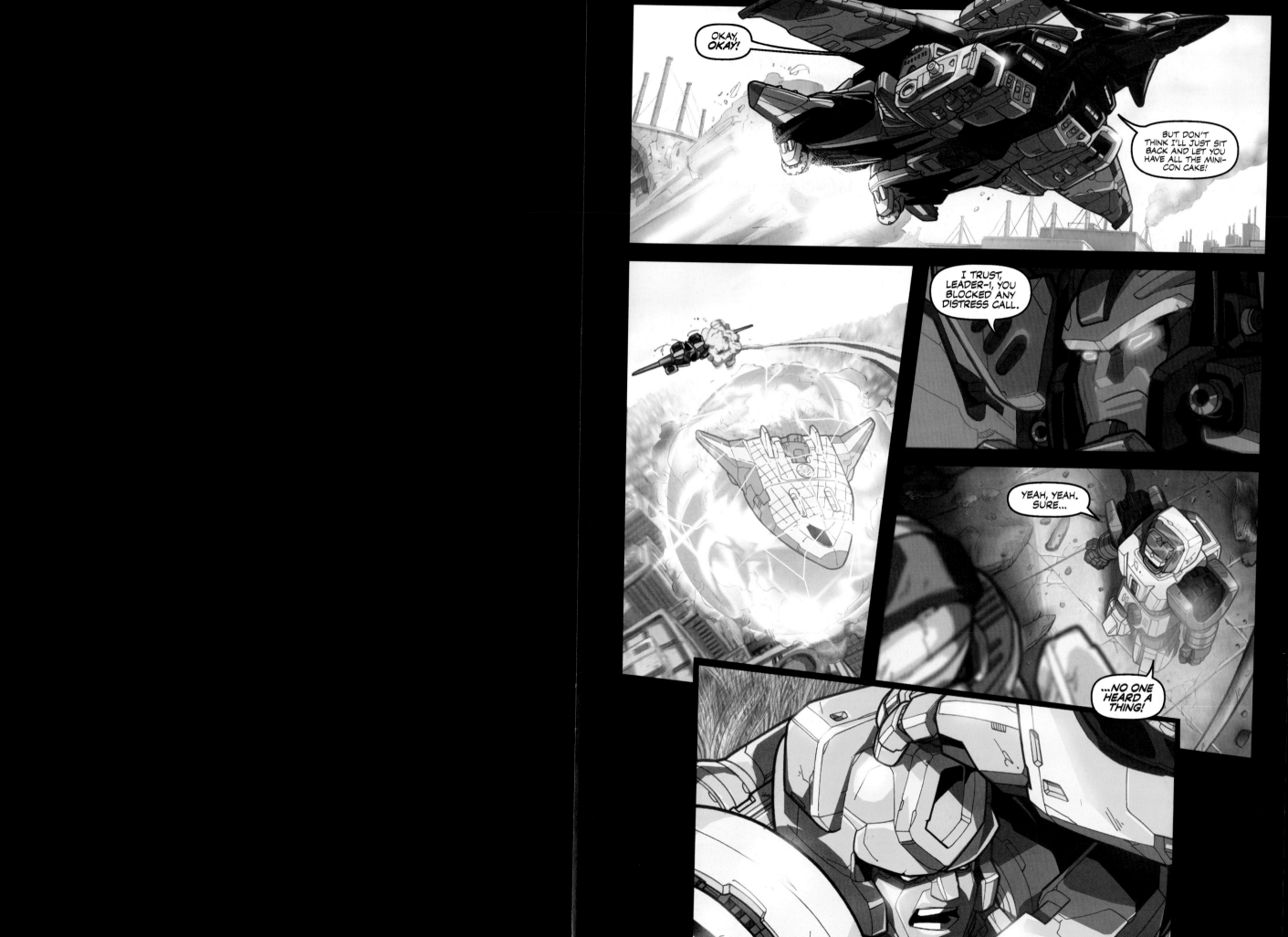

THE OUTSKIRTS OF LINCOLN:

TIME I GOT THERE, MEGATRON AND THE OTHERS WERE ALREADY WELL WITHIN THE SECURITY PERIMETER.

I COUNTED *THREE* MINI-CON CAPTIVES...

...BEFORE THEY *SPOTTED* ME.

AFTER THAT, IT WAS EVERY FLYING CAMERA FOR HIMSELF!

AUTOBASE:

MHM. THE DECEPTICON STRONGHOLD IS HEAVILY FORTIFIED. A RESCUE OPERATION WOULD BE OUT OF THE QUESTION. THIS IS *BAD*.

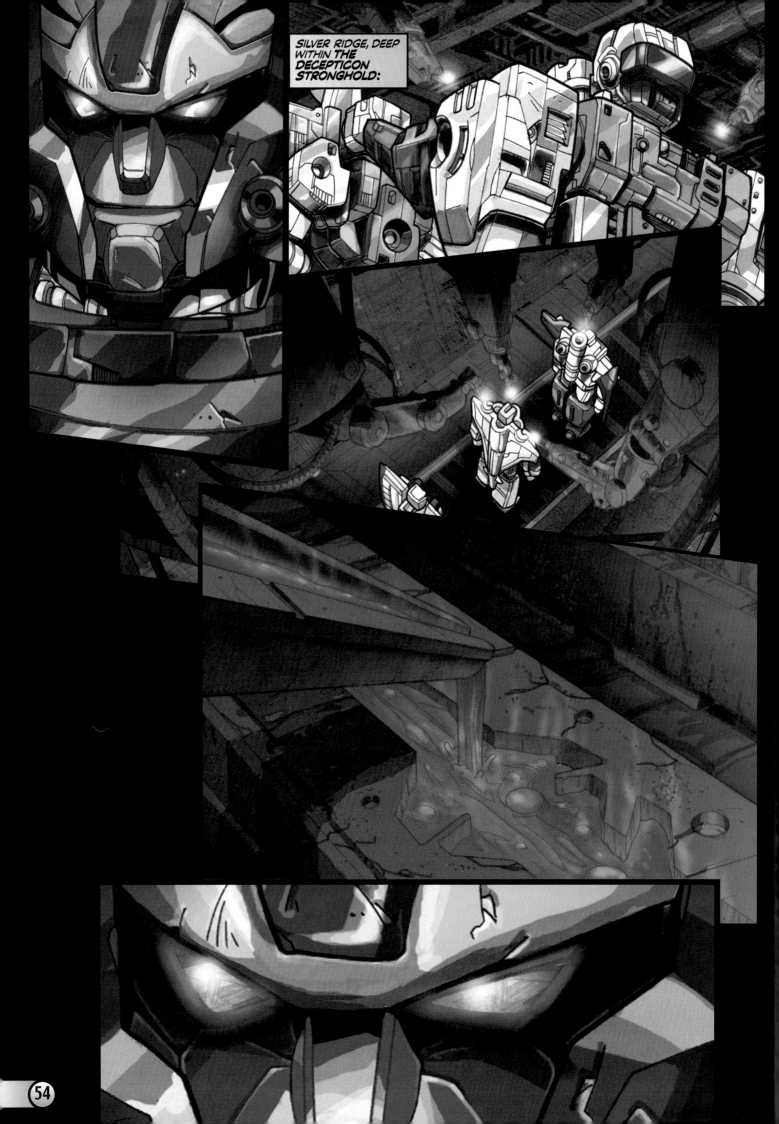

SILVER RIDGE, DEEP WITHIN **THE DECEPTICON STRONGHOLD:**

INSIDE...

THINK! THERE'S GOTTA BE A WAY TO DEEP SIX MEGATRON'S PLAN, OR AT LEAST--

TOOM!

EH?

ITCH!

WELL... ...HELLO!

BLAST-- THERE WASN'T SUPPOSED TO BE ANYONE *DOWN* THIS FAR.

SCATTER! USE THE LOW COVER...

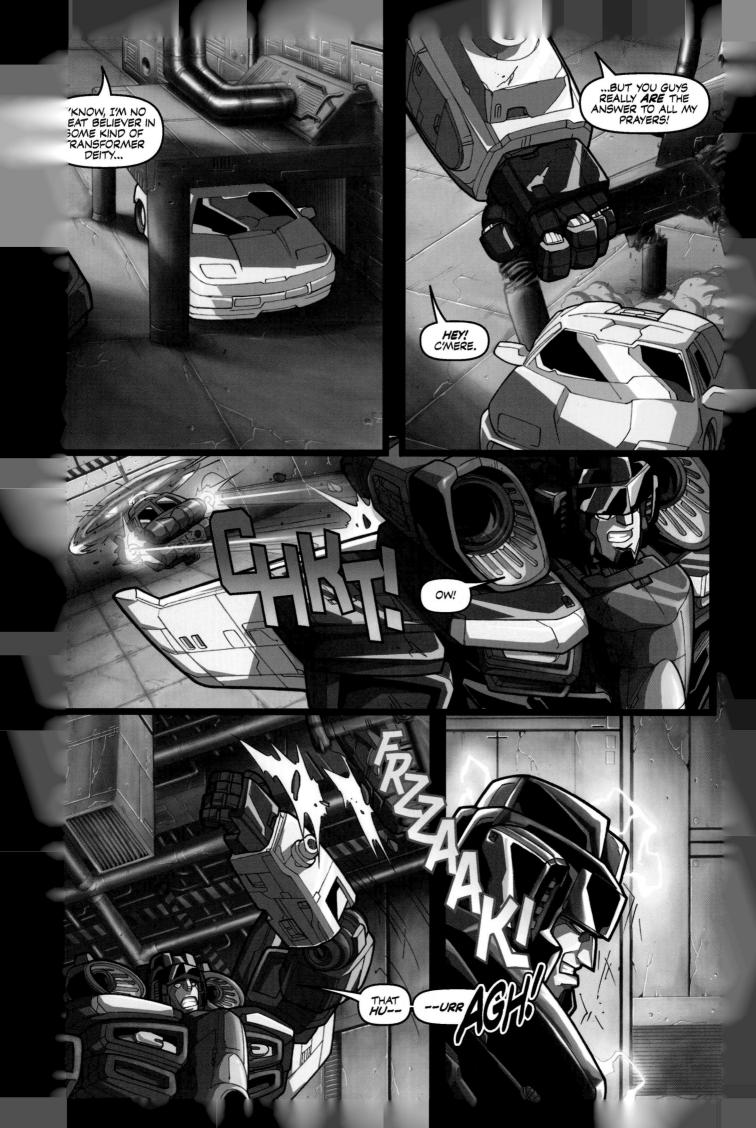

BTOOOM!

OH...

NO! LONGARM-- *BACK UP.* THIS WHOLE THING. IT'S GOING TO--

...HECK!

NEARBY...

MORE...